Hope in Hateful Times

Molly Ann McDonough

Brigid's Books

Published by Brigid's Books.

Cover design and illustrations by Molly Ann McDonough, including the false rose of Jericho (*Selaginella lepidophylla*) on the front and the rose of Jericho (*Anastatica hierochuntica*) on the back.

Title: *Hope in Hateful Times*
ISBN: 979-8-9948141-2-3
Printed in the United States of America

For my dad, who wrote me my first poems of roses and violets,
and my mom, the muse I wish every daughter had.

Roses are red, violets are blue
Here are some poems for you
I hope my verses bring you joy
Let's create more than we destroy

Foreword

The morning comes in as tracks left the night before in a newly fallen snow. You can partly tell where the critters have been, where they go, by the direction of their prints.

On a clear day there is sun and a deep blue sky with thoughts of warmer days still to come.

There will soon be rain fresh on April's tilted fingers—the ones that touch roses, feel the wind, and the damp coming of spring.

Flowers will bloom, lovers will fall in love again, dancers will twist and twirl under the light of the moon waxing full, wolves will howl on some distant plain.

Tiny streams drink their fill, grow to larger streams, move in search of distant rivers. Alongside the moving water, small plants also point toward the sea.

New bullfrogs sing love songs and the whole earth wakes to such wonder ways. The wind in new leaves joins the great bursting alive songs.

Honeybees search flowers, measure distant ways, tell others, tell their queen, tell the coming day.

In the quiet of the morning, a new poet comes on the scene on the little blue planet deep out in space, a swirling sphere, speck of life struggling to be. The poet will see things others fail to see, will record things not yet heard and bear witness to things that are strange and wonderful and full of delight and sorrow and joy.

She will form paths not walked, plow new ground to open the earth, look for ways and whys of the universe where the little ball sails on a journey too long to quite comprehend.

Such is the poet Molly Ann McDonough.

I met Molly a few years back at the annual Imaginarium Convention in Louisville, KY, where I was presenting a poetry workshop and Molly attended. I was immediately impressed with her work, which I felt was some of the most promising in both prose and poetry that I had seen. I have followed her ever since and she continues to impress.

Now comes her book of poetry, *Hope in Hateful Times*, and what an interesting collection it is.

Let me give you a few examples to show what I mean:

"Panicked senses search feral
For panthers in the tall grasses"—*The Extant Ever Waiting*

"You can feel guilty for anything you do
Even more so for everything you do not"—*The Extant Ever Waiting*

"If I were the first bright sun of spring, I'd seek out your face
If I were a spider, I'd adorn your forlorn corners with silk lace"—*Alive*

"I am wild like flowers beloved by bees
And I am wild like the open seas"—*The First She*

"Crunch, crunch, crunch go my feet on the forest floor
My prints the only hints anyone has been here before"—*Shinshin*

"When I can taste awe
In ripe apple flesh like Eve
Bursting sweet on a tongue
Full of belonging
Full of desire to Know"—*Worship*

"Around our sun we joyously danced and swirled
Then joining once more, we formed a whole new world"—*Star Matter*

That will give a hint as to what to look forward to in Molly's work.

I do want to mention one other poem in particular. It is called *Tits Out* and is exponential in its development of human experience. It is a virtuoso of prose poetry and one you do not want to miss.

I introduce you to Molly Ann McDonough and say it is a clear bet that you have not seen the last of her. She will be around awhile.
So join her now on a journey, perhaps you have not been on before.
Get ready for the wild wonderful ride ahead.

—Lee Pennington
Named Kentucky Poet Laureate by the State Legislature in 1984
Louisville, KY
February 6, 2026

The Extant Ever Waiting

Your pulse spikes with peril
Breath turns to gasped ashes
Panicked senses search feral
For panthers in the tall grasses

Star-glazed death waits to pounce
On you, a rodent in the dirt
But fear is yours to denounce
Gather your resolve, mind alert

And stand.

Long legs unfold, spine uncurls
Wide predator-spotting eyes on top
With claw-clasped end absent, fear unfurls
But your heart rate doesn't drop

Moonlight illuminates no lithe severance
But maybe mountain shadow hides
A more pernicious malevolence
Your shadow tugs, sucks, stills your strides

Perhaps this reticence saves you pain
From something unseen and unknown
Colorless, odorless, breathless methane
Creeping through cracks in mine-scarred stone

Rush back the way you came
From this undefined, not-quite-fear
Though it feels near the same
Senses stretched, silence stalks near

Hairs on the back of your neck rise
Once again, look over your shoulder
Sure this time to find slitted, yellow eyes
But you're hunted by something much older

Search your body for insight
Sure this sense has a name
The deep knowing that all isn't alright
Could this feeling be shame?

But no. We conquered shame
Long ago. We beat it as a nation
All as one, self love we proclaim
Pride pervades each subpopulation

We're proud of our identities
Our cultures and histories too
We're all perfectly ego-backed entities
You're exactly as proud of me, as I am of you

But if not shame, what presses near
Eager to breach the bounds of your skin
Caresses like a lover most insincere
Still your lungs against horror seeping in

But breathe you must, though the next may kill
Bar your lips to the extant Ever Waiting
Too soon your ribs expand against your will
In flows life, in flows the night invading

Whispers from your mouth, "Thanks for letting me in."
Recognition echoes from all your hollows
All this time you ran from not-so-original-sin
But with this knowledge, no relief follows

Yes, you know this sense very well
Shame and Fear's third evil stepsister
Unmentioned and left to wield her spell
With name unspoken, how could you resist her?

Guilt.

Memory stretches back for when you first met
She smiles as your mind runs dry
Perhaps she's been with you from the outset
Snuck in with your first screaming cry

Or did she join as your mind grew?
Soak with you in the water of the womb
Passed down from primordial mothers to you
The unchallenged, original invasive bloom

No one warns you against the natural order
She lives in every mother, sister, and other
They say it's best to just absorb her
With enough practice, you'll forget you suffer

You can feel guilty for anything you do
Even more so for everything you do not
Guilt for unmet aspirations you pursue
If you meet them, guilt races ahead uncaught

Guilt for feeling worse than the best
Guilt for feeling better than the least
Guilt for feeling guilt when you rest
Guilt for feeling guilt released

You're guilty until proven innocent
But there's no time for court proceedings
Best keep your head down penitent
Assuage your guilt with daily feedings

Till she's so constant, she's sunk into your marrow
She says with your voice, tired eyes narrow
"Why don't you chill out? Take a breather.
You're such a spineless people pleaser."

Shifting Seas of Self

Get comfortable
Feel your hands on your knees
Your weight on your chair
Gravity connecting you to the earth

Focus on your breath
In. Lungs, stomach expanding
Out. Stomach in. Throat constricting

Go deeper
Into the depths of you
Active in your thoughtlessness
Keep your waters still
like glass
In.
Out.
Again.

Feel around
You're bigger on the inside
An expanse of emptiness
of unexplored territories
A map marked "here be dragons"
Venerable valley of déjà vu
Don't look too close
Slumbering malevolence might
stare back at you
Race to the safe sunshine of
soil your soles know

Here the home where you loved her
Occasionally you visit
Clean and open the windows
Plant bright flowers in their boxes
Swap out the dusty, sunbled drapes

A grave, yes—
but not a profanely forgotten one

There the painstakingly built pyramid
peeking through trees
Once a step-pressed path
Now you don't care to visit
Precious stone spoliated
Copper wire stripped
Not even a tomb

More recent monuments
Cities surround
Expand and contract

So many relations and roles replaced
or left vacant
Are you even still you?
The same ship though every plank supplanted?

Yes.

Still the sea through every shifting tide
Still the desert though dead dynasties
hide beneath your wind-carved dunes

You.

Your past wouldn't recognize you
Or perhaps it would

You.

Rise up through your mind
Feel your body
Open your eyes

Alive

If I were the first bright sun of spring, I'd seek out your face
If I were a spider, I'd adorn your forlorn corners with silk lace

As the frost, I'd release the grass under your feet first
As the rain, I'd fall to quench your thirst

As the fading sunset, I'd hold on tighter
As the stars, I'd shine brighter

As new growth, I'd sprout prouder
As newborn, I'd scream louder

A warmer breeze
More thriving bees

Afternoon teas
Easier ease

In reaching for you, I'd shake off my dust
As every brightly beating heart must

Where you walk, weariness wilts and dies
My friend, you are so wonderfully alive

Liminal Love

"Lovers embrace that which is between them rather than each
other."

Sand and Foam
        - Kahlil Gibran

The same sun blesses us, but
I am the redwoods gazing down
At you, the glistening, roiling sea

You sing for me in curls and crashes
Foam crests mailed on moonbeams
My limbs creak as I reach
Against the steady stretch of my spine
Bearing my pines away from your spray

I sink my roots into your rocky shore
And you breach my soil with your brine
To find your essence can't caress mine

They say you can never truly know another's soul
And perhaps they are right
But how could I behold your beauty
Your boundless chaos-swirled cycle
And not try to know more?

So on the thousandth
          Or trillionth
                    Or infinith
Night of your cliff-echoed call of
"Meet me on the shore, my love"
I sink knotted joints into eddied groves
Rip back my gnarled bark
Gash into green growth
Peel sapwood smooth and pliable
To carve myself a new form
One that can embrace you

You who spent eons breaking
Yourself upon the rocks in yearning
Craft coral bones, and abalone eyes
As fast as lightning striking your surface
To emerge shining, dripping on the stony shore

Our first touch is an end of longing
And the barest hint of its beginning
Your arms hold me closer than warm soil
Your eyes see me clearer than cloudless skies
We whisper into each other's mouths
"I will spend a thousand"
          "Or a trillion"
                    "Or infinite days learning you."

We fill dull beach with beautiful moments
Bright pebbles and polished sea glass
I bend for a round, flat rock
Smooth and comforting in my hands
Placed the night you welcomed my boring jazz with
"*All* jazz is boring. That's why I like it."

Beside it, a seafoam green sea glass from when
You received the delicate gift of my favorite poet with
"I understand why you like her. She's perfect."

Stepping on our smooth stones with bare soles
We come to those shined by the sea
There a showy deep red shell
From when I agreed to love
Your favorite philosopher not despite
But because he was a petty, arrogant asshole

Wade through waist-deep waters
To the shadowed cave where we stored
Our traumas in broken brown bottles
Time-smoothed into something sacred
As the wind sings through these shards
I'd never bare to another, I wonder
Do we truly not know each other?

Return to lie entwined in the sun
Let it dry the salt to our skin
Next to us, lie some of our first stones
Paired pieces of pink quartz that say
"Love needn't be permanent to be true"
And "My love will never be a prison"

Our shore shines with a rainbow of reminders
Of those first truths
And more
Whelks that whisper, "I want you."
Stones that state, "I see you."
Glass that grants, "I get it."

But still, there are small gaps
Between the press of our palms
And the wind caresses your sacred voice
Before it reaches my ear
Can the language of the sea
Be the same as that of the trees?
Would I know what was lost in translation?
What sizzled away into the steamed air
Between your thoughts and mine?

Don't I have truths buried at depths
Even I won't dig to?
What shadowed corners of your soul
Won't you share?
Secrets kept for shame, or fear of harming me

You've always made me feel beautiful
Brilliant. Wanted. Seen.
But it's possible you silently want
Someone less ancient and more brave
Less focused and more free

But no.
My insecurities, my loneliness
Do not fit in the liminal space between us

You placed every stone on our shore with me
We formed every fern, each blade of grass
We wove the winds, and sculpted the lands

I know how our seas taste on your lips
How our trees dance in our rains
How the fine hairs of our arms
Glide with our grasses in our winds

I may never know you, or another, or myself truly
But I live in the world our love built

Altar of Adoration

I'll worship the space between your hips
Whisper my praise into your lips
Draw out unearned guilt from within
And lick the shame from your skin

Bite into the apple of my flesh
Emerge from my holy waters fresh
Make love without bonds or restraint
We've no original sin to taint

Our bodies separate the sky and land
Between us burns no hellfire-backed demand
Create a universe between your arms and mine
Don't need God's forgiveness because, mercy, you're divine

You, me, and our altar of adoration
Aren't a Trinity that deserves damnation

Perfect Forms
(AKA Greek Philosophers Can All Suck Eggs)

I confess, I've wished my legs were longer
Words like *willowy* and *graceful* would fall from smiling lips
But they're the perfect length to wrap around your hips

I'm sure if my waist were smaller
Admirers would admit they love hourglass women best
But my belly's the perfect place for your head to rest

Perhaps it's silly to be joyful in a world growing ever harsher
But my hope doesn't feel like a weakness
When slipt prettily between your nihilist fear and stoic sweetness

Each soft skin-pressed whisper reassures
Maybe my form is perfect when pressed against yours

Lil Beefcake

Heat gathers beneath my skin in a dim room designed for sweating. Contorting into ridiculous shapes, the negative space where joy of movement and escape of everything a woman's body must never be meet. Yoga girls don't normally look like me. They are slim steel scales balanced at attained goal weights. I bet if you placed all the comments telling them to lose or put on pounds on either end of a plank, it would poise perfectly on the fulcrum of their downward dog. But not the girl next to me. She's shaped like me—short with thick curves of muscle. *She's a Lil Beefcake like me.* The thought explodes in my mind, both sudden and familiar—a firework that had always been there, growing in the warm, moist soil of my subconscious to burst into pyrotechnic bloom.

A Lil Beefcake.
Like me.

Class begins and I match her push up for push up that the teacher says are optional. But the choice between aching arms and disappointing my fellow Lil Beefcake is no choice at all.

Later, in a locker room sauna, the voice of a lone older woman greets me as heat from an open oven door. "I'm always so jealous of people who are shaped like girls." I freeze in this furnace, unsure if I should thank her for saying I look young, or womanly. "With those hips and legs. When I was young. I never had any shape. My mom always told me I was too thin. Well I guess now I have these." She looks down at her bathing-suit-clad breasts like a caved in cake. I say I think she has a lovely shape. A girlie shape. She tells me how then she got too big and spent the last several years losing weight, monitoring all the food she eats and mold she breathes, trying to find a doctor who would listen, and how she's never, at any size, liked her body. I'm her girl-shaped priest in a sweaty sports bra cassock. We need no screen to hide us in our cedar confessional. No woman is ever truly separate from another's hatred of their body.

In a corrugated metal farmer's market barn on the first unseasonably sweaty spring day, I sit at a booksellers table with three other female authors. Between the slow, sharp swirl of the industrial ceiling fans and the public restrooms, we discuss our writing and lives and the right amount of eye contact to make with strangers. At lunch, I eat the second half of a bagel sandwich I started at breakfast. The author next to me yells, "You're eating again?" and when the other authors turn, startled, "She's eating again!" One replies, "Let her enjoy her metabolism while she's young," preserving the sacred peace of my final meal before my metabolic processes get the electric chair. I want to say, "I'm thirty-five, not sixteen, and I work out six times a week" to defend my audacious choice to feed my female form. But the shame cycles back to their own bodies, a clockwise fan drawing the hatred up from our sagging skin and widening waists. They speak of how much weight they've put on. How they're heavier now than they were during their pregnancies, as I quietly chew my bagel, like a Lil Beefcake. Later, I realize I only saw one of them eat anything approaching a meal in the six plus hours we were there, and I wonder if female metabolisms do inevitably slow down—playground merry-go-rounds with no more girlish legs to spin them—or if our bodies eventually get used to slowly starving.

I am conventionally attractive. I know I'm not supposed to admit I'm aware of it, but I don't see how I could not be when it's the first, most consistent, and loudest truth the world would like me to know about myself. I am beauty defined in negatives. I'm not as fat as I was, nor as muscular as my mom fears I'll become. I'm not showing my age...yet.

I'm not so tall that I'm intimidating, nor so short that I'm an accessory —six inch stilettos serving to show I'm still smaller than a man. I'm white. But not so white that my shame easily flushes my face, that love bruises linger on my neck. I am told almost daily how lucky I am for everything that I lack. How dare I complain about the boulder of arbitrary, impossible European beauty standards bearing down on me when I'm not yet crushed by it? How whiny, weak, annoying to admit anxiety when I have it as easy as it gets. But I can't help but wonder why even female compliments frequently come with a side of shame, a plate one of us must clear before we can leave the table. If this is as easy as it gets, why does it still feel so hard?

I listen to audio creator Helena de Groot talk to poet Vievee Francis about her upcoming memoir, Ugly. That's the title she chose for her life story—Ugly. She says that she battled against the truth the world wanted her to accept for many years—that her black face is ugly—but that she has lost her battle against body dysmorphia of her face.

Body dysmorphia.
Of her face.

The phrase calls to the hatred I have buried in all the expected places. The soft rolls of fat hidden under high waisted pants. The cellulite on my thighs. It springs to my eyes as hot, freshly-horrified tears. We are expected to hate aspects of ourselves. Our noses, smiles, skin, hair. To not would be an unacceptable level of arrogance. But her entire face? Vievee says she's accepted she'll never see anything but a monster in the mirror. That she'll never be cured, but she has started to be capable of enjoying clothes if she thinks of them as costumes. Helena says that after recovering from anorexia from fourteen to her early thirties, fashion will probably always feel too painful to engage with, but now, in her late thirties, she's beginning to feel the intensity of her self hatred cool. They agree that late thirties is a better time to stop hating oneself than mid fifties. But late thirties is when I'm meant to start hating myself. Earlier really. I'm already living on borrowed time. Prepaid minutes bought with every comment comparing me to a child.

And of the two options, it's an easy choice. I'd rather be a biological clock with the sands of my worth draining inexorably through my hourglass waist. Would rather spend every moment waiting to turn into a grandmother clock, clanging "Enjoy it while it lasts" at every passing girl that needs to prepare for her fate, than spend every day tossing kindling on the fire of my self hatred until I'm just too old and tired to fan the flames. But I don't understand why it's a choice of when we must hate ourselves instead of why we should at all.

Vievee explains, "All women are put under the wheel from the day they're born, and it's crushing." Her statement is a match to a fuse buried in my mind for thirty-five years, igniting twin fireworks of realization that obliterate my confusion.

> 1. It feels hard because it fucking is.
> 2. This is why women are constantly
>   filling each other with shame.

We can't let the wheel catch us unaware. Felling us at the shins, knees bent backwards, hips separating, pelvis splitting. If we shove each other down first, pressed as thin and small into the dirt as we can, reinforced with dense shame within—when the wheel rolls over, maybe we survive.

Helena says that looking at her sister's body, which is shaped like hers and is beautiful, helps her to see herself not as beautiful, but as less hateable. Vievee agrees that she loves her sister's face. Constantly wants to kiss her aunts' and nieces' noses. And I realize that grouping myself with my fellow Lil Beefcake has made me like my belly more. Has released some of my guilt around eating gluten. Because would a Lil Beefcake worry about the calories in a pint of beer, or her shoulders getting too muscular? No the fuck she would not.

My face isn't losing what it should be, it's becoming more like my mother's, my grandmother's. My shining, curling grays match the tinsel in my great aunt's Christmas tree glam shot with her beehive hair, martini, and grin. Our bodies are matriarchal. Made for sacred casseroles, caloric cocktails, and decades of collective joy. If we must always compare ourselves to one another, then let the links be beauty instead of shame.

We can all be Lil Beefcakes.

The First She

He says I'm not feminine enough
My hands and words are too rough
Worth in decline since eighteen
Wit and incisors are too keen

But my form's not for his delight, it's my own
My nature's not his to condemn or condone
Won't be fit in a box for viewing pleasure
I will become at my own leisure

Not frozen as maiden with demure blush
Quick smile, never angry, posed in pretty hush
Not defined as endlessly selfless mother
Only sexual when a womb used by another
Nor rezoned as crone with wisdom to extol
Once beauty is lost to covet or control
I am all of these and more
I am after and before

I am wild like flowers beloved by bees
And I am wild like the open seas
I'll prettily defy man's plans and neglect
Steal his fear if he won't give his respect
I am creation that brings all new life
And enveloping darkness that ends all strife
I know not the first goddess's or cosmos's name
But know She and I are one—the same

Garden of Me

Man wants me soft, open—easy to wound
Scar tissue exfoliated away by nightly ritual
Potions caress to worship my youth
My elasticity and resiliency

Man wants me easy to till into neat plots
Endlessly productive yields for every crop
Any unsanctified growth pruned
Through daily devotion

Man wants me clothed in ancient flame-weathered bark
Walled off for rest from a warring world
Peace and protection so they can
Rebuild and re-inherit the earth

I did not bore rebar into my spine
To support man
Nor adorn my skin with glass shards
To protect man
But to survive societies that would carve
Me into easily consumed pieces

And when man's wars recede
I do not relearn my softness
Revitalize my salted soil
Remove the sharp glass from my surface
Leave the crumbled gaps in my stone
For man's ease of access

But so pollen-brushed petals won't
Tear against my whispered words
So furry paws can pad safely along my mossy walls
So laughter can swim languid through my skin

I did not adopt this form for man's comfort
I will not change for man's convenience

But your love blew as dandelion fluff past my walls
To lay your tired brow on my sweat-moistened soil
With your bloomed promise of "love is not a burden"
You became mine to nourish in all your softness
What poisoned soil would starve a Spartan weed?

Feminine Rage

Women are the emotional ones
Ruled by ebb and flow of the moon's passions
Men kept rage, tossed the rest into women's ocean
Everyone knows male anger is a rational emotion

Women are the gentler, milder, weaker gender
Prone to hysteria if not treated tender
That's what they say, anyway
But here "they" means "men," always

Women need protection
But only men get consideration
Male-only crash tests and studies for medication
Religion centered on men, as is the entire nation

If women are emotional, it's understandable why
But the stereotype still seems like a lie
The emotional woman isn't a phenomenon I've seen
I've seen women with no boundaries so as not to seem mean

Women who can't accept a compliment as every attribute is expected
Women accustomed to constant guilt for every flaw yet corrected
Women so careful not to offend that they unlearn to speak
Women that suppress grief to not seem weak

That shove everything down into a tight little mass
To suppress all the problems they've heard women have en masse
All to be more perfect mothers and wives
Though intimate partners are most likely to take their lives

Most likely to take labor and give abuse
To trade her lifelong dreams for their lifelong use
Men are 6x more apt to leave spouses with deadly prognoses
Women receive 80% of autoimmune diagnoses

To find out why, doctors collect statements for case study:
"I knew in less than two days my husband wouldn't be there for me."
"I nursed him through cancer. When I got MS he cheated with a family
friend."
"Doctor, you're the only one who listened to me up to my very end."

Unmarried men are sadder, unmarried women are the happiest
population
But they speak of women as a burden, despite this information
So when the risks are great and the benefits doubtful
Women should be anything but pretty or palatable

Why strive to be dutiful wives and mothers
To give up pieces of ourselves to be peace for others
When they've defined femininity to mean invisibility
Measured female worth by the ability to sustain crushing responsibility

What does it mean that even in a poem on female rage
My first concern is how men will perceive my words on the page?
What of men who work hard to give their wives the lives they
fantasized
And stayed by their side when their feminine rage metastasized

But just this one time, why couldn't I think of women first?
Instead of once again getting the fraction reversed
First and foremost, we all know it's not all men
But secondarily, it is all women

All women have been raped or feared that they might be
All girls were given half the aspirations and twice the responsibility
All females were told they're "not like other girls" or saw it in a movie
All ladies are taught to expect less no matter how unassuming they be

But what if I still do want all those feminine things?
Am I weak, programmed, or letting my ovaries pull the strings?
To want to be pretty and caring, with nature and family in tune
To want to be a lover, a mother, and a wild goddess of the moon

Maybe if we were all selfless and kind the world would be better
We could stop short of self-sacrifice if we strived together
One day, I'll release the emotions stuffed deep in my ribcage
In the future, I'll emote without shame and heal as I age
But today, I'm taking back my feminine rage

Domestic Creature

Does anyone know how to clean out a toaster?
Opened the crumb traps and shook all the ways
Still hear crust rattling—clean isn't any closer
Give up and hope not to start a fire with toast strays

And no one can fold a fitted sheet right?
Admit "I've just been balling them flat," while my mom stares
She responds, "yeah I can see that," like the sight is a fright
But non-Euclidean shapes don't fold into squares!

Unmet messes plague like myriad maladies
No matter what I do, there's always more laundry
Ancient abominations acquire life in shadowed alleys
Of my fridge. Daily life is a quandary

My dad says I was never domesticated
Like I'm a raccoon roaming free
Instead of domicile-strapped, society-weighted
Wildly exploring doesn't sound too bad to me

But still the slight cuts—I'm somehow lacking
Mom says she was never very domestic either
When she sees my feral smile cracking
How does one become domestic, when born a wild creature?

I'm really good at cleaning when there's time
If I've the hours my meals are beautiful and nutritious
My interior design vibe is cozy and sublime
And my holiday pies and cookies are delicious

Mom makes a lasagna better than any I've had
And can fix the dishwasher when it breaks down
Drew up an addition for our house in CAD
Does the plumbing, electric, any repair around

From foundation to roof, she could rebuild
And while I'm no Sandie, I'm not bad
At painting, drywall, and cement I'm skilled
What aptitudes do we need to add?

To have that domestic je ne sais quoi
Martha Stuart still a symbol of poised class
Despite serving jail time for breaking the law
Pass Snoop the blunt, then hold Homey Mass

Maybe it's not what we lack in the home
But that we look comfortable without
Allow our bodies and interests to roam
Instead of bowed in the kitchen devout

We should seem like a teacher out of class
Something awkward and uncomfortable to behold
Out in the world belonging bold and brash
Instead of bending into the smallest space we can fold

Until you barely see us in the scenery of our domain
An easy smile aproned in servile flexibility
Grandmother afghan faded into familiar terrain
Maybe domesticity is a synonym for invisibility

Worship

When youth and beauty
Age and comfort
Lust and joy
Are all things to
Fear and shame

When cleanliness is next to godliness
And god can only fill me if I am
Small, still, silent and empty

When my eyes must be downcast
My ribcage corseted
My fingers clean and folded—
How could I ever hope
To touch the divine?

But when I can sink soft hands
Into warm soil
Keep crescents of cycling life
Under my nails

When I can worship like the bees
Pollinate velvet wildflowers with
Lustful fingertips

When I can drink in joy
Like a languid cat
Lounging as liquid sunlight

When I can taste awe
In ripe apple flesh like Eve
Bursting sweet on a tongue
Full of belonging
Full of desire to Know

When I can float with starfish
In a sunset sea
Prideful, humble, complete
An ever-yearning drop of immensity

When I can hear, smell
Taste, suck
Touch, shiver
See, adore
Question, learn, know
A world so full of beauty
I must eternally expand
So we can continue
Spilling into each other

Then I can be reverent too
From my grass-brushed toes
To my cloud-drenched gaze—
I worship

Spring

I changed the shape of me to fit you
Love that once rang happily through us
Clangs through me with a horrible resonance
Screams along my faults—jagged edges I break into

I'm certain the birds joyously announcing spring
Do so to spite ears that ache with your absence
Sun bursting through clouds with brilliant incandescence
Flames in eyes that find all beauty lacking

All my favorite songs abrade abused nerves
The only tolerable sound the rain's outrage
Arms wrapped tight around my ribcage
To keep from spilling beyond my body's curves

I inhale in desperate anxiety
Sure my crushed chest won't dilate
But HUUUUH—My lungs inflate
WHEEEW—And empty
Again, to make sure it wasn't an anomaly

HUUUUH
WHEEEW

Sun-floated memories of perfect harmony
Of flamingo-pink summer night bliss
Gentle waves of your sea-salted kiss
Are now abhorrent to me

How can buds still be on their branches
And there—my pants still on the floor
Right where we left them before
My mess outlasted all our chances

Curl into myself a little more
Hold on tight to what remains
HUUUUH—Air expands my core
WHEEEW—Out it drains
Again. I got through this before

HUUUUH
WHEEEW

Surely the world should be rent in two
Land seized with seismic shocks
Time violently torn into separate epochs
For when I did, and now no longer, have you

But no.

The balloon you got me is still floating
The candle's flame has outlasted ours
Still perkily in their vase are the flowers
All painfully prod with spiteful gloating

Time moves on as if nothing has changed
Its refusal to stop or jolt forward a betrayal
The ground insists on remaining stable
I'm the only thing that's rearranged

Oh, if I must
Shoulders back, chest outthrust
HUUUUH—It comes easier than before
WHEEEW—My next breath isn't uncertain anymore
Again, with the fresh spring gust

HUUUUH
WHEEEW

I suppose the ephemeral buds do have a certain charm
The winds bring Mother Nature near
Did the air used to be this clear?
And the sun on my face isn't doing any harm

The rains don't sing with sadness but renewal
To pink and purple clouds the showers retreat
The earth is warm beneath my feet
With arms stretched wide, join chirping birds' approval

HUUUUH—Maybe spring should come again this year
WHEEEW—Perhaps there can be beauty without you here

Tits Out

I

Warm salted water tumbles me like laundry to land. I swim back out unafraid. Wave after wave buoys my eleven-year-old body. It's my favorite week of every summer—visiting my great aunt at Myrtle Beach. On the shore, my mom waves with her whole arms, cups hands to mouth and screams something. I spin, searching for sharks. See none. My mom points to her chest. I look down to see my bathing suit has slipped—nascent vigilance leaves budding breasts exposed.

During sun-drenched departure in my great aunt's shimmering purple and turquoise golf cart, my mom reenacts the scene. Pointing at her boobs and waving. Harmless laughter at how long it took me to notice. At how carefree I was, careless. How unaware of my new parts. But I hadn't thought much about them—beyond that they gave me somewhere to hang a string bikini. No one told me how those grownup triangles of fabric might displace my dignity. As she's still pointing, and laughing, and waving, a passing golf cart of teenage boys waves back to her boobs. I laugh at her instead, glad someone else's body has been exposed by capricious waves.

keep your new body
secret—shameful inside joke
no one shared with you

II

On the hazy school bus home, my friend and I play with a kid's meal toy. Sixth grade is too old for toys, so we indulge ironically. A boy sits on the bench beside us. Perhaps offended that life still allows us play, even ironically, he reaches across my friend and grabs my tit. Turns my joy to shame. I brace my hands on the brown pleather bench backs and swing my legs over her. I slap at his face and head and shielding arms with both hands. I try to kick him in the dick for good measure. My mind hovers above my body—a list, push-pinned to corkboard of all the places I've heard it hurts or offends to hit another. When the shame groped into my body has been struck back into his, I sit back down between my friend and the window.

The bus driver returns to school, makes him get off. He cries. When I walk down the aisle at my stop, all the other children clap for me. I'm filled with pride that I defended myself—with gratitude that my first sexual assault was such an uplifting experience. My dad asks why I'm late and though I tell him I handled it, he makes me show him the kid's bus stop, ask my friends in the neighborhood which house is his. No one answers when my dad rings the doorbell. I wonder what he'd have done if someone had. The boy never rides my bus again. I wonder how he gets to school. It isn't until adulthood that my mom tells me my dad screamed at my principal until he put him on another bus.

mind your bodies, girls
never-ending vigilance
starts before first bleed

III

In college, I sit on my dingy black futon, in my sparsely furnished living room, with a new friend after a night out. He's drunk enough to share about his disabled mother and touch-starved childhood. I'm drunk enough to hold his hand, though I've told him I have a boyfriend. We fall asleep watching Phineas and Ferb on my laptop. I wake up with the hand I held plundering down the front of my jeans. My first dry-mouthed thought is that I must have somehow consented to cheating on my sweet boyfriend, who waited patiently for me to release my virginity from Christian clutch. But his hand is in my panties and we've never even kissed which feels like the wrong order to cheat. So I kiss him. Bring him into my bed to sleep away the rest of the morning.

For years I feel guilty about cheating, until I see him on Facebook posting the sweet surprise rooftop dinner he's made for his girlfriend—complete with fairy lights and white pillows—and I realize—he assaulted me. She probably doesn't know her boyfriend has assaulted someone. Does he, when it took me so long to accept he violated me? When I was friendly with him after? Maybe another woman has since taught him it's wrong to reach into her body and steal her choice while she sleeps.

maybe your body
will never be yours
when you're so careless with it

IV

After undergrad, across the country for an internship with an aerospace test lab, I go on a dinner date. Afterwards we walk on the dark, desolate beach. He kisses me—hard. Doesn't listen to my polite objections, see my body language, feel my hands pushing at his chest, as he forces himself on top of me. I calmly contemplate if I could get my phone out, dial 911, before he noticed. How many steps I could race down the beach if I took him by surprise. Enough to say where I am and why I'm unsafe? Fresh from boot camp, he'd overpower me no problem. Is he more likely to attack me if I announce he might? Would he risk the career he's launching with a rape accusation? Logically, it's not worth it, but do potential rapists listen to logic?

Eventually, he lets me lead us back to our cars. Probably never thinking how close I came to bolting, that his heedlessness is a threat. I wonder what it means to be so at peace with my powerlessness—veteran of not being safe in my body.

stand up for yourselves
but don't be bothersome, girls
resist politely

V

In my thirties, after I've suffocated all the obvious children of my Christian guilt with lace and latex, sweated out purity culture with partners good and bad, I meet a man who always asks. Asks if he can kiss me. Asks if he can remove my shirt, my skirt. Asks if he can touch me. Asks if I'm okay while he's inside me. And I learn I can say when I'm uncomfortable before counting to thirty in my head and hoping they cum first, sixty if they haven't. My body relearns what safety feels like—slippery, silly, and vocal. That it's something planted together, given air and light between us.

I still have a voice
my body can be mine first
we share each other

VI

In monthly massages for persistent middle back pain, my masseuse says I must work on my posture. I excuse it as "normal—better than a lot of women's." She rants about how "girls are always taught to hide our boobs, and it's terrible for our backs." She tells me, "Stick your tits out."

I imagine I'll feel seductive standing boldly upright. But the first few days of constantly reminding myself to peel back my shoulders from around my chest, I don't feel like I'm saying, "Look at me, boys." No, my posture says, "Fucking try me, bro." Like I'm ready to fight again. And maybe that's what chiseling my spine from the shame it's curled around is—a daily battle.

let our bodies take
the shape our proud bones planted
stick your tits out, girls

Doña Quixote

I don't want these modern loves with terms and conditions
Donned my "ride or die" t-shirt so all can see
I'm on a chivalric heart-sworn mission
I'm the Doña Quixote de la East Tennessee

When I moved my unwashed king into my castle
Friends asked "but wouldn't a professional streamer make money?"
If anyone hassles him, I'll give 'em a wrastle
I'll fight the windmill of their negativity

He's my prince and these boiled hotdogs our feast
I don't need an errant night with my Dulcinea del Toboso
My old, cat-scratched couch is our noble knightly beast
Stay home to watch him game, where else would I go?

Express my devotion in 430,279 words
Summarized since my dove isn't much of a reader
As would you be one of those pitiable pragmatic lords
Or an earnest fool for love that believes life sweeter?

Ick

I love him, and that's all I need to know
Don't need him to post or publicly show
He doesn't work, but that's okay
I've got enough to pay our way

He doesn't know how to take care of his health
I'll make his doctors appointments myself
Yeah he drinks a lot, but is it an ism?
That's just judgement passing his light through a prism

He's only 5'6", looking cute in his hemmed jeans
But he no longer seems to care about my dreams
Says his last girlfriend was easier to make cry
When my friends and family ask how it's going, I lie

We go to the gym together, he can't have me getting fat
But why is he using the elliptical like that?
He's so bouncy, a gazelle running from a lioness
Maybe his jerky knees were more made for idleness

Oh.
    ...oh no.
        ICK.

Has his head always been shaped that weird?
Yikes—I just pictured it without the beard
Grab my phone, check a photo to see
Do I love an ugly man who's not even nice to me?

I wish he'd take his sunglasses off the back of his neck
He leans in for a kiss. I turn my cheek for a peck
Why does he clench his butt like that when he walks?
Jesus Christ, pick one—chew or talk

How dare he act superior to my interior design
When his is the boy version of a "Live, Laugh, Love" sign
His "taste in music" is whatever shit happened to fall upon his ears
He wants to seem secure, but won't stop with his basic bitch fears

How can he be so boring and still not interested in me?
He'd be better off absorbing my personality
Watches, cars, and sad boy tunes are all that's there
I need to take a breath, I'm not being fair

I love this man, despite this new view
Lean in to try again... but actually... EW.
The love of my life has transformed into a pathetic prick
There really is no coming back from the ICK.

Skin-walker

My masseuse tells me my body feels like it needs to dance
             to move joyfully
This differs from her saying where I hold tension in my back
             that I need to stretch my lats
                    stand up straight
                           stick my tits out
I imagine when she touches my skin
she can feel the capitalist electric hum of
fluorescent tube lighting buzzing within
Like still working at midnight
             and still not being enough

I dance a little in the car on the way home
             but I have no venue
                    no community
                           no time
to dance the way my body really needs
Sweat rolling down my back
If I'm really feeling the song, myself—
wearing the goofy millennial dance-frown
none of us can seem to keep away

Limbs moving with rhythmic assurance
not that I look good
but that I don't care
       because my body
           and my friends
               and the drink fizzing in my throat
                  are all a hive
Moving in honey, salty synchronicity with the
       Queen Bee of the Universe
          and everything is alright
          and it always will be

Months later, I tell my masseuse
sometimes I apologize to strangers who are rude to me
It makes me furious that my first instinct is to shrink—
rush to restack the comfortable social expectations *I* didn't kick over
She is shocked by this
Says I seem like I'd stomp someone—that I could
I say thank you
She says there is something that needs to break out of me
like I'm a werewolf that needs to tear open to release my true form
The buzzing beneath my skin must've grown
       to joints popping
          threads snapping
             fabric and skin tearing

She says she'll figure out what kind of skin-walker I am
          I say thank you
That there's something animalistic about me
          Thank you
Something kind of sneaky—prowling
          Thank you
She says I'm a panther
          Thank you

Long before she said that
I'd fantasized about reincarnating as a cat
Sometimes as a house cat
alternating between naps and snacks
between kisses and cuddles
Digging my claws into flesh just because I'm comfortable
Having a household of suburban human staff to serve
Killing only when I want to
as a reminder that I'm still faster than a snake strike
even though I sleep all day

But sometimes fantasizing about being a wild cat—
a panther even
Black fur warm and shining in the sun
Shoulder blades cresting with my silent slink
A roar that rolls like terror
down the spine of every vertebrate
A body that runs like rapids
Jumps like water over falls
Rises obscure and ominous like fog
looking down on my domain
Then curling up or sprawling out
into the most comfortable nap anyone has ever taken
Because sumptuous repose is easy with a spine
made of water

I bet panthers don't get back pain
But stretching as a panther—oooof
Imagine it.
Paws spread, claws extended
Would it feel like cracking your knuckles?
Like bending your fingers back
        till the tendons stretch through your palms
                and your hands forget they've ever sent
                    an email in their entire lives?

Know the way a back that's never bent over a desk can bow—mmmm
Always ready to stomp a fool
Not because I lift numbered weights in numbered sets
Not because I asked ChatGPT
            the right grams of creatine and protein to take
                    to finally be able to lift my own body
                            but not so much that my face gets puffy
                                    and my jeans cut into my stomach
But because my being is just built for balance
Made for rest and death and play
Clothed in unconcealed cruelty

Can I have that in my human pelt?
Can I admit some creatures deserve my cruelty?
Can I dig my claws into what I want to keep?
Not just a little—
            leaving tiny crescents of desire on bare back
                    but not breaking the skin
            sinking teeth in shoulders to mark my claim
                    while concealing my jaw's ache to consume

Can I rest without guilt?
With such comfort that sunspots seem made to warm me?
Can I let my nature move me?
So when people touch me
            they don't feel it roiling and ravenous
                    ready to split me open
                            and claw its way out?
Can I let this body be animal?

Shinshin

Crunch, crunch, crunch go my feet on the forest floor
My prints the only hints anyone has been here before

Warmth wrapped close with wool and down fill
My red-tipped nose alive with the chill

The woods look safer blanketed in snow
Under clouds of white, sharp holly tips show

Tufts float from trees in the breeze like cotton
Birds sing of new life, buried but not forgotten

A snow-lined vine provides a splendid seat
Crystals sparkle in the sun around my feet

The wordless woods dampen my voice to quiet
Stillness settles my mind's clamorous riot

Chapter Book

Prophesied orphan take my hand. Lead me through liminal lines from literal to literary. Discount Books separated by slivers of time from being an AutoZone, a Mattress Warehouse. Through the forgotten wardrobe to dusty basement library shelves, through a train platform wall to the band of light spilt from hallway to bedroom floor after bedtime. Pull me between pages so precious that though the bookstore, the library, the home and light are no more, the stories still live along our spines. Though the magic *maybe* of childhood letters and fairy godmothers has long slipped through my fingertips, I still see the enchantment of silently sun-dappled old growth, of porch-wrapped summer night thunderstorms. A broken bottle, older than me, the oldest child archeologist, unburied in the backyard with all the careful fervor and stored with the secrecy fitting a find of its magnitude. A favorite family photo in vacation brights, framed just beyond the border of my memory. A thousand half-forgotten stories live in the shadowed corners of my smile. As one, they still whisper *whimsy*.

taped-together spine
Scholastic Book Fair antique
make-believe heirloom

Hope in Hateful Times

For Refaat Alareer

My hope used to reside in safe suburban homes
Sacred shelves kissed fantasy to legacy
Reassuring statistics bound in academic tomes

Increases in life expectancy and literacy
Genocide a gladly extinct horror of history
Devastation washed away by democracy

Society as a global symbiotic system we
Built over centuries. Slow march towards morals
Not perfection, but steady progressive victory

Built on hope in just Supreme Court quarrels
Hope in public services and sustainable designs
Hope in protections for coastal corals

Hope in wine grapes on sleepy summer vines
Hope in everything in mind and sight
Hope in soft grass cut in gas-scented lines

Hope as a given—a birthright
Hope that held horror as aberration
Hope that slept soundly every night

Until the bombs bought by my nation
Dropped on home, hospital, and school
Months of silence and lies from every news station
Daily firsthand footage of the unimaginably cruel
Years of impotence from international organization

Not the end of progressive peacekeeping rule
But wide-eyed exposure it never existed at all
Tear-raked reckoning that I'd always been a fool

As I watched the UN and ICJ fail their claimed call
Leaders yielded everything except the status quo
Liberals hid behind false cause and care cinder wall

Each silence dealt my worldview a city-crushing blow
But when forced to sacrifice my humanity or hope
I could not numbly hide from the horror I now know

So death to my lifelong, all-encompassing hope
Death to kind, summer-sun-kissed world
Death to any shared morality's scope

Death to faith, around mankind curled
Death to joy, with shameless charms
Death to sleep, peacefully unfurled

Death to babies in their mother's arms
Death to every bearer of a family name
Death to ancestor-rooted olive farms

Death delivered by bombs with precise aim
To poets, journalists, surgeons with impunity
Whole cities to rubble with the victims to blame

Endless relocations with no safe community
Surgeons lucky to be released with crushed hands
Others found dead in starved and tortured nudity

More killed at home with their entire clans
Drones play kids' cries to lure saviors into fire
Death count rising from tens to hundreds of thousands

Are you still listening?
Can you hear the shattered sound a mother makes
Over her murdered children?
Can you see a father carrying pieces of his
Baby in plastic grocery bags?

Have you cut off your shock?
Beat back your empathy until
Anyone who dares to care is a threat?
Have you buried each unforgettable horror
Under the weight of historical genocides?
Did you wrap "that's just war" as a
Comforting scarf around your currently safe neck?

Don't.
Not yet.
We haven't even gotten to the worst part.

Which is—there's no point.
It's all for nothing.
It's not to keep your team in power.
Or a more dangerous one out.
It's not for economic stability or border security.
It's not divine will or retribution.
It's all because of one brutally senseless truth.
One you already know, even if you don't admit it.

The psychotically selfish are in power.
Not as exception, but as rule.

Gluttonous oligarchs with bloated boots
To global throats can stroll easy because
Another tread is primed to grind
Our bones into the ground.

There's no one person to blame
So all can hide behind our closed eyes.

Collectively blind to every atrocity
Nightmare upon horror upon war crime
Each new worst thing I've ever heard
Blurred into a heart-dotted Instagram scroll
An endless, bottomless pit of suffering
Social media appeals and aid donations
Tossed into Tartarus
Along with the world I loved so well
Along with all the tender pieces of my being
My love
My will
My care
Until I am stripped bare
Alone in bomb-ashed, tear-salted soil
Waiting for whatever will
Reclaim the broken earth
Forsaken Job, still alive in a world that's
Watched all beauty burn

People say my smile has changed.
I can't make it reach eyes filled with agony.
Eyes raw with sleeplessness
Because my mind won't leave
This waking nightmare.
A heart without hope beats
Apathetically beneath my bones.

But then.

An appeal from the deepest pit of hell.

"Help my parents, my siblings, and my grandparents first."[1]
Brave sandal-clad men clear rubble with bare hands
A little girl wearing a big, red bow returns hell-birthed

Hope tied to a white kite over death-covered lands[2]
Hope rising from the ashes of its former abode
Hope as a cracked concrete weed that withstands

Hope in shoeless child bearing brother down dusty road
Hope in starved woman breaking stale bread for the birds
Hope in hurt teen suffering to ease injured dog's load

Hope in aid workers risking their lives to serve
Hope in doctors ducking bullets to reach their patients
Hope in unarmed kids facing fascists with pure nerve

Hope that galvanizes this generation
Hope not in votes, but in tenacious tides
Hope in protests and outcries from every nation

---

[1] Twelve or thirteen year old Alma Jaroor called this to rescuers from under the rubble of her home on December 4th, 2023. The rest of her family was killed. https://www.aljazeera.com/video/newsfeed/2023/12/4/girl-under-gaza-rubble-asks-rescuers-to-help-relatives-first

[2] A reference to Refaat Alareer's poem "If I Must Die," which went viral after Israel murdered him. He is the poet and professor this poem is dedicated to.

After receiving death threats at a UNRWA shelter from the Israeli military, he fled to his sister's apartment. On December 6th, 2023, Israel killed him, his brother and his son, and his sister and all three of her children. On April 26th, 2024, they killed his eldest daughter, along with her husband and newborn son.

Hope like a freedom flotilla glides
Our eyes grant safety through seas of insanity
Hope that looks to Indigenous guides

That take pain as a reminder of humanity
Grief as love with nowhere to go
And put it into strengthening our community[3]

Take illusory permanence and search below
Shake off the powerlessness of being alone
And know, together we can grow

Not a gentle uprising the establishment condones
Not discomfort measured in dollars and days
But resistance that builds a world better than any known
A current that through generations boldly says—
"Nothing will remain in the valley except its stones, and we are its
stones."[4]

---

[3] The entire stanza paraphrases a post made by Leah Manaema who works through an Indigenous lineage of anti-oppression. https://www.coculturecommunication.com/

[4] Written by Dr. Adnan Al-Bursh in his final social media post. He was a highly respected Palestinian orthopedic surgeon and head of orthopedics at what was Gaza's largest hospital pre-genocide. On December 5th, 2023, he was abducted from a hospital along with other medical staff by the Israeli Occupation Force. In April 2024, he was delivered to a prison in the West Bank where fellow hostages say he was left injured in the prison yard naked from the waist down. On April 19th, Israel announced his death with no cause. Human rights organizations corroborated signs of torture, severe beatings, and possible sexual violence.

Our hope will be like the sun's rays
Not always felt, but always returning
Nurtured by and inspiring countless displays

Of bravery, love, sacrifice, and learning
Reclaimed languages and passed-down keys
Every reforged soul joining our sea of yearning

Alive in hearts holding agonies along ecstasies
Root in reclaimed lands with olive seeds sown
Plain when stood proudly, and when forced to knees

Like a lightning bug, illuminate the unknown
Let basil flower on your balcony for bees
Love every vulnerable joy you've grown

In hope we are indomitable, never alone
Try as they will—they cannot kill stone

Star Matter

We were the star matter of a newborn sun
Together we burned, together were undone
For endless, untold eons, we churned and changed
Down past the smallest atom, we rearranged

We became small, dense, and then utterly spent
Violently crashed apart in dying descent
Carbon, nitrogen, hydrogen, oxygen—
We flew apart as the building blocks of men

Our light extinguished, we raced through the dark sky
Past neighbor stars and galaxies, we sped by
We slowed our atomic pace light-years away
Basked in sunlight again, we resolved to stay

Around our sun, we joyously danced and swirled
Then joining once more, we formed a whole new world
We aged and grew as we twirled around our sun
We broke into creatures to fly, swim, and run

For a time you were big, and I was then small
We lived thousands of lives, then forgot them all
We forgot what we were, and from where we came
Each life changed our aims, but ended just the same

I was a part of five hundred apple trees
I nourished you as a thousand sucking bees
We fell with the rain, and with the earth we dried
We rode on horses, and also were the ride

We crawled, climbed, clawed, and cluttered
Slithered, stretched, stalled, and stuttered
I fought, flamed, framed, and fluttered
You met, missed, made, and muttered

We went extinct, and were the first of our kinds
Alternatively closed and opened our minds
We discovered, lost, rediscovered, forgot
Gave credit where due, took it where it was not

We cried, crumbled, came, and claimed
Mothered, mustered, manned, and maimed
I touched, tumbled, tried, and tamed
You numbed, nurtured, neared, and named

We hunted down our future for our present
On the aims of few, the lives of many spent
We waged countless wars, and fought on either side
Each, like the last, seeming wholly justified

We hated each other with each changing face
We hated by species, we hated by race
We destroyed, and leveraged, and destroyed some more
Held grudges, and of each wrong, kept careful score

We killed, and ignored, and watched out for our own
Crushed under lives and eons, we were unknown
From our planet self, we took without thank you
We tried to warn us, didn't trust we told true

We turned water to waste to power our play
Instead of *me* and *us*, we said *it* and *they*
But the next time you kill me, or I wound you
Remember we're the same once these lives are through

We were born as one, and lived billions of starts
And the same star matter makes up both our hearts

MAIDENMOTHERCRONE

is a braided poem written collaboratively by
Kayla Nichols and Molly Ann McDonough.
It is also published in Kayla's debut collection,
The Stuff of Stars.

I
with sleek hair and perky breasts
that spill out of your hands
and exist only to nourish
not yet your child but your fantasy
a true maiden seeks to be sought

Early frost of men needn't freeze
Soft petals as demurely alluring bud
Father sun says bloom as you please
Pieces of you will die in the mud
More will grow, knows mother tree

II
with humble heart endless patience
that flows from bottomless well
and shepherds babies with your eyes
into and through your world
a true mother serves others

Your breasts swell to nourish
Your heart and biceps grow to hold
Not fairy godmother to everyone's every wish
Their story of us smokes with power controlled
Love, soul, home flame in you to flourish

III
with sexless body and generous wisdom
freely given to rising generations
and tongue bitten to avoid
offending breadwinners
a true crone slowly disappears

The end of fertility is no death sentence
Release the cycle of blood and pain
Step into your natural ascendance
Mother or no, leading by love is your domain
Each sparked spirit is of crone descendance

named for that which we give
The souls that usher every life to live
what are we
if not vessel for seed
You are universe
Stars of creation freed

The God of Moments

Maybe in the future we'll have the god of air purification
The goddess of plastic refinement
Twin gods for the fluoride in the drinking water
And the Great Pacific Garbage Patch in the ocean

The way we used to have gods of harvest, war, and love
Things that you could dig into
Things that could kill or save you
Redemption revamped as prefab structures
We can integrate into our inorganic world

Religion nowadays has fatally fucked up
There's nothing in it to burn your incense to
All sacred scent stripped in the monopolization
The globalization of modern monotheism

He's the god of us and them
But what if we want to kill them?
He's the god of the entire universe
When we're just barely seeing beyond our stars
And what of any green, big-headed alien invaders
Is he their god too? A male homo sapien in a flowy robe?

No, in being the god of everything
He's lost anything that matters
In being the god of holy wars and manifest destiny
He's stopped being the god of grandfather olive trees
Of dandelion beards and children growing old

When the empire falls and we choose anew who we'll bow to
I will name the goddess of a lawnmower on a hot, quiet afternoon
Of morning cinnamon rolls that smell like every parent, not just yours
I will whisper prayers to sun shining on my napping cat's fur
Build altars to honeysuckle eyes meeting mine across humdrum rooms

I will worship the god of the breath after this one.

Question Your God

I wasn't there when your world broke apart
Didn't witness faith in family and god depart
But I can guess how it went for you
Because I went through it too

First you notice there are quite a lot of religions
They convert the world to war zones with their divisions
Each battle is between good and evil
But which is which? They all just look like people

Our courts and churches wrestle for control
Fight for individuals' and the nation's soul
But if I want my religion to be protected
Doesn't theirs also need to be accepted?

How do I know the beliefs I was born into are right?
No one seems to be listening when I pray at night
Because I have questions, has god turned away?
But they say he created me this way

How can I be a worthless sinner and in his image perfect?
How can three be one? They're not equal last I checked
Why would an omnibenevolent god create both good and bad?
Why does unconditional love have so many conditions to be had?

I wouldn't want anyone I loved to be tortured eternally
To feel guilty for thinking or for who they are internally
Is it love to demand someone's entire life for your use?
I read about narcissism, and it sounds like emotional abuse

Maybe these beliefs don't benefit me, maybe they never did
Perhaps they've been nothing but a burden since I was a kid
When I distance myself from them to see how I feel
I don't sense god's absence, just space to heal

The world is so much lovelier focused on beauty to try
Than praying to avoid sin while I wait to die
I can love so much better without hell hanging over me
Is that how it felt for you to break free?

Did you regain your guilt when you shared your liberation?
Did your community taint your truth with old doubt and hesitation?
When you look around freed from religious hate
It doesn't change the state of problems or lessen their weight

They'd still control us by supposed god-given right
Kill each other when it's climate change we must fight
Instead of creating a fair world to leave for the next
Focus on forcing strangers to have the right kind of sex

It's so stupid once you're free that you don't feel free at all
Now you're more appalled than ever to watch the world fall
All for some shared delusion, and not even a fun one
Hate their whole lives in hopes for better once they're done

I can't fix this world or say what happens after
But I can share in your bitterness, hope, and laughter
We can hide together when global suffering is too much
Press back the world's cruelness with gentle touch

Only time can take the taint of religious guilt
But I can value the beliefs you've built
I can kiss your tears and try to understand
I can love you without lifelong demand

ACAB

For the police of East Tennessee

"All cops are bastards" is what they all say
Confident chants condemn absolutely
Announced by Antifa with covered faces
"Back the blue" counters drown out the story

A week ago, got my first speeding ticket
Caught in a 55-45-55 trap
After seeing cop cars at each limit change
Blame belongs squarely in my own lap

Angry jokes about downloading dating apps
Cycle through profiles until I match a cop
Agree to meet and then stand his ass up
Because he got someone on a bullshit stop

Assume from the squad cars lining the streets
City has a smaller budget than before
And to not downsize or demilitarize
Bastards are out stealing from the poor

After we laugh, my friend reminds me
Cops are always way worse than you fear
As our mom and pop town suffered no cutbacks
But paid $28 mil to rape victims this year

A serial rapist roamed free for decades
Corrupt cops took payouts to make his excuse
A drugged woman fell from his fifth-story window
Bastards at last had to search his den of abuse

Attorney as bait at bar where he preyed
Cause she asked they stop granting endless escape
Arrested him for illegal ammunition
But ignored numerous rapes he had on tape

Actually had a "Raped" list with 22 names
Cops said, "Maybe that's what he calls sex. We don't know."
And, "She's dressed like a real—well, I won't say it," on the
Black dress of the woman pushed out his window

Attorney who pressed them got fired, not answers
Cops wouldn't talk to the women on the "Raped" list
Assault charges already pressed were ignored
Benzos in their blood were also dismissed

Arrested and allowed to escape again
Cops' accounts filled with shady cash infusions
A half mil missing from the rapist's safe post search
But was evidence reviewed for legal conclusions?

Absolutely not. Hard drives and devices
Chronicled drugged rapes of 70 women and kids
Abused attorney begged to put pedo away
But he kept raping as they ignored her bids

After two years conducting business openly
Cops "caught" him exactly where she said to look
And were the corrupt, callous cops fired?
Bet you can guess which direction that took

Actually promoted to lieutenants and chief
Course that $28 mil came with non-disclosures
And stealing it back from citizens in tickets
But don't assume guilt you suspicious supposers

And even if all our cops are guilty
Can we condemn over a million lives?
Abuse is four times more likely in their homes
But that leaves 60% with unbeaten wives

A cop's widow tried to spread the blame with—
"Cause there are bad firefighters too—that's a fact."
And then got real quiet when I responded
Bad firemen don't shoot kids in the back

A killer cop is 25 times more apt to go free
Cops are now cammed, but is the record button pressed?
Atlanta found 40% don't comply, but they'll
Beat protesters and charge with resisting arrest

Abusers in big cities and small towns
Caught with their knees pressed against our necks
Always with their hands in pants and pockets
Beat us, then pay us with tax-funded checks

Are all cops bastards though? I really
Can't say. But they are worthy of loathing
All are fucking class traitors
Bourgeoisie collared dogs in wolves' clothing

Burn it Down

For Bob Vylan

All this dissent in the streets, no one wants to work anymore
Husshhh—lower your voice
      act civilized
           admit it
                you only hate the rich because you're poor

We buy the factories and move production offshore
Bought the public transit, and swiftly closed the doors
Sssshhhh—come hear boardroom secret—if we demolish it,
      they'll go to where the jobs are

Calm down, we'll sell you a car
Let's check your credit score
Shame—our records show, you've not borrowed here before
And what's more—
      your income falls below how rent's trending
Try down the street, there's a Northern Star Lending

Yes, we'll pay you what you're worth, we always have
Struggle is a sign you're simply overspending
Sure you can organize, but do it legally and peacefully
And make sure not to disturb anyone or anything
      Less than thirty silent people
          on third Thursdays
            at three pm
          is what we're currently recommending

Nah, you know what?
Fuck that—let's burn it down
Burn it down
Burn it down
Call the National Guard to town
Rip plywood off the Tesla store
Even the credit score
Not blaming our class anymore
In the ashes, freedom's found
Let's burn it down

It's really the immigrants you should blame
Yes, we killed their leaders
        and to their gold laid claim
So maybe
        if you want to nitpick
                it is our fault they came
But they're so much easier to exploit
Instead of pay, we can just give ICE their name
In business, one must be adroit
It's a shame, you wouldn't understand
But you need bargaining power to make demands
What's that? Unionize?
        You think you can fuck with us—ask Detroit.
                Ask the democracies we've overthrown.
War makes cheap fingers work to the bone.

Actually, wait—the Indigenous are to blame
If they'd just give us their last strip of land
We could grant jobs fracking for oil
I know all you do is toil, and never your own soil
Alone with no space to even be alone
Women these days just aren't loyal
It's the Republicans
          Democrats
                    Blacks
                              Whites
                                        That must atone
The Christians
          The Muslims
                    The trans athletes
                              The misogynist podcasters
They're coming for your rights with the judges they appoint

                              While they're busy fanning flames
                              Pointing fingers like fucking clowns
                              Let's burn it down
                              Burn it down
                              Burn it down
                              Spotlight from face to face aims blame
                              But the system in power remains the same
                              Now's the time to stake our claim
                              Stand our ground

Solidarity protects the poor
No class infighting anymore
Stop letting us all drown
To save corrupt crown
Burn the rot to cleanse the ground
In the ashes, freedom's found
Let's burn it down

Unconditional Love

Created in your majestic image
Given voice and knees to worship
Empty my fleshen vessel
Flood with your unconditional love
Carve out my worthless nature
Purify my cavities with holy water
Dig deep to my original sin
Till my cavernous center
Echoes your voice back to you
Remake me each morning
Consume me as an offering
The lamb slashing
Its own throat in sacrifice
Help me atone any aspect
That is not you
Absolve me with your righteous fires
Burn away the weakness
Of my soul
Until my scars shine with the Holy
Light of your reflection
Borrowed bones pressed to dirt
Essence entirely consumed
Separate from the rest of your creation
Able to abhor all that is created
By and yet not of us

With omnipotent intimacy
Finally emptied
Righteously ravenous
Ready to consume eternally
All beings back into our
Unconditional love

Land of Milk and Honey

The fertile crescent
  Land of milk and honey
    A god's chosen place
      For his chosen people
      Blessed by birthing his most
    Beloved mortal son
  Soil anointed by his blood

  Soil turned to salted ash
By his chosen children
  All beauty razed to rubble
    Babies vaporized by bombs
      Or left to slowly starve
      Returning small bones
    Visible beneath taught skin
Back to ruined earth

May gods never come
  To my land
    May the cosmos stay silent
      And men be born deaf
        For I have seen how
        They worship

The Magic of Maybe

"If you're going through hell, keep going."

I stopped believing in evil when I stopped believing in God
The world made me believe again

Capitalism has corrupted its host like a cancer
Killing kids in cobalt mines so we can watch
on the latest tech as we kill others in their beds
Then in their churches
Then in their tents
All so the most parasitic people alive can have more

But on those same cruel screens, I've seen a teen
take the bandage off his own wound
to help friends catch and wrap a dog's injured leg

Is it enough that kindness emerges from the rubble
of unimaginable cruelty?

My eyes shine like Christmas lights
when I see the first snow of the year
My voice sings, "It's snowing!" to anyone near
My thoughts roll like bright ribbons
My arms wrap like red paper
Through crisp air, love calls clear

Is it ridiculous to be full of joy over common
crystals cold enough to kill?

Death seems to come in December
This year, waited welcome from the family cat
Abandoned forest spirit my brother found thirteen years ago
Too weak to walk or eat much by the end
Death is never dignified, always devastating

But he spent his nights in a new bed my sister mailed
in the glow of my dad's sacrificed space heater
My mom folded for daily devotion on the floor
because he could no longer follow
but never liked being alone
My dad told me to take him on a walk outside
because nature guardians can't be cooped up
When I showed him the cold-dimmed trees
the winter oblivious bamboo
the hills he used to watch over
sheltering his skeletal body against my chest
to try to share my heat—he purred
I didn't know he still had the breath to purr
So we took turns taking him on walks
holding water bowls and small bites of food to his mouth
He took his last breaths in my mother's arms
and then we all dug his grave together
I don't know why I thought I'd have to do that part alone
but my mother wouldn't even let us look as she lowered him

My first poem was published when I was ten
It was about my friend who got shot in the head
and all the things my elementary school mind
mourned her not getting to do
Learning to drive
Going to prom
Growing up

But once I watched my mom give the actual shirt off her back
so a dying woman could feel pretty
I plan scavenger hunts inside when the
world is too contagious to go out
and my neighbors bring each other soup
whenever someone's sick

My second poem was published at thirty-five
It was about sexual assault and the way the
world wears the fight out of our bodies
But a man I only met once messaged me to say
he read my words and they made him cry at work

I cried the other day reading Jane Eyre for the first time
and then obsessively read nothing but Brontë books for weeks
Their words reach hundreds of years into the future
to say that though their lives were short, and sick, and brutal
they were also stunningly beautiful
There are so many astounding things to read and write
Experiences that tie our souls together
and attach our lives to this world

I'm still meeting new best friends in my thirties
I hope to still find profound loves in my nineties
My cat cuddles into my arms
when I go to bed and when I wake
In the winter the sun sparkles on the snow
In the summer it shines in streamers through my eyelashes

And maybe, if we keep kind
If we keep going
We'll be alright

Interstate Neighbors

Can't cut these blind curves too fast
A rollercoaster carved into cliffs
older than bone
Seldom is the road whose speed limit
can surpass your will to race
That's okay
Put the windows down
Feel mountain freshness on your face
Leave curls of your summer songs beneath
blue sky breaking through verdant boughs
Drive by slow enough to see

clean white wooden siding
Butter yellow shutters buttress windows,
bright flowers in boxes,
plastic lemon wreath on the door,
brick chimney puffs away chill
A small home, but enough to raise two kids
that always got along,
even as teens
As adults, the kids visit often

Three hammocks hang from oak boughs
to encircle the trunk
Parents in one,
children in the others
White wine in stemless glasses,
bare balls of feet pressed to bark
Laughter fertilizes soft grass,
white picket fence borders,
no "Private Property" sign needed
for tragedy not to trespass

Gone in a lavender-lilted blur
The wind wails at clear skies
Trees whisper warnings in a language
long lost, but known in your spine
Speed drops to 35
A stretch of road you'd rather not slow for
Side streets trying to return to forest
form the perfect spot for a speed trap,
but this area is forgotten,
even by deputies, throwing tickets
into the mouth of a starving budget,
in a dying town

Peeling paint,
sagging shutters with slats defecting
slant from dark windows
Creeping vines the only visitors
Rusted vehicles litter the lawn,
planted in high browned grass
Depressed porch piled with debris—
permanent, jarring, constricting
Rasped, echoed smoker's hack
will reside with them till they die
The plaque of depression has crept by
plentiful "Private Property" signs
to harden this place's arteries

Down to 25 through a small town
Half fast-food restaurants,
half changed, reclaimed
A courthouse-turned-YMCA
An old brick building holds a hairdresser's sign
that calls your childhood to the surface
along soothing swerves of nineties fonts
You don't know how these towns survive
Don't stop to find out, yet
can't help but be charmed
as you accelerate to 55

Double-wide trailer,
arthritic hands tend flowers
in cheerful corners of the yard
Only child chose to end early
The unimaginable, come and gone
but they remained—
a love story in the end
Two Adirondack chairs,
sat armrest to armrest
Smiling over mountain sunsets,
sometimes counting yellow cars going by—
a sweet tea nightly ritual

You'll never know them
They don't know each other
And though the news says the name is extinct
Neighbors all the same

Pittsburgh Microburst, July 1996

Paint, plaster, framing pine, cinder block, siding—separate each suburban silo. Incessantly cut grass outlines plots blessed by bank paperwork. The occupants of each unit are relegated to different rooms, populated by the artifacts of their distinct realities. White walls, blind windows, business suits, perfume bottles, enveloped bills, and time ticked in red alarm gashes distill adult domains. Pastels, bold wallpaper borders, favorite shirts now a size too small, toys turned to clutter by a parent's gaze grant child ones. Regularly scheduled programming on staticked screens tunnel vision into commercials screaming consumption. Outlets buzz, fridge hums, dryer rumbles, air-conditioned tiles freeze bare feet, parents get home too late, street lights wink on too soon, "MOM look at this" goes ignored, dinner broccoli makes a prison of plasticked mahogany, term measured in time taken to force cold mush from mouth as tears stain face, then tucked sheets tie bonds of bedtime—and how could you sleep with the TV laughing and voices murmuring and the house still breathing and the cicadas clacking alive and your feet are cold and your body is hot and your tag is itching and the wind is whipping and the branches are creaking and trees are slamming and then—it all stops.

Trees crash through rubber ropes—break apart the poles. Fragile order fizzles. The house sighs and sleeps. The wind, the neighborhood, the machines, still. I wake to a dark, silent house. Parents spin up battery radio to announcement of midsummer snowday from work. Unfold bright chairs in the driveway. Gather ice, fridge food, and drinks into our red cooler. Inside turned out. Neighbors spill into our space. Parents' secret days melt into our play along asphalt-heat wavering chalk lines. Pops of coke cans and sour-smelling beer spark against laughter and bike bells and adult talk which is boring but exciting because it's here, in the middle of the day. Grilled party foods on paper plates replace nightly trial by vegetable. Bedtime feels late when we've played together all day. Inside calls us into cocoons of candlelight, family moving in warm yellow-orange circles of hide and seek. There's always been candles. Big column of white wax behind box of etched glass. My small plum in a smell named Merlot with its beaded butterfly holder. Decorations dimmed by dust come alive. Make magic adventures of shower time, swimming pool sun sparkles of shower spray, shadow puppets of shampooed hair on shower curtains. Me and Mouchie, my cat named after the neighbors' cat, cuddle cleanly into bed. I wish I named her Merlot. I pray the power stays out tomorrow. Drift to leaves laughing and bugs buzzing. Wake to no alarm snoozers or lawn mowers. Another day of togetherness. Of outside and sun and grass and summer. It feels endless and temporary like summer vacation and I want it to stay this way forever. I'm happier this way and so are the parents. They say they miss coffee machines and air conditioning. Laugh at me when I ask why it can't stay this way and say they have to go back to work. But they're smiling instead of yelling. Playing instead of cleaning stuff no one cares about. We get another full day of perfect climbing branches and whirling wheel-spoke-beads. Of soft grass and warm bare feet and cold cooler water and the driveway turned into a slip-n-slide by hose and tarp. But after three days, the world rumbles back to its routine.

Decades into my own routines of paying bills, of snoozing cell alarms; of perfume bottles, office politics and reading between the lines— power outages pull me from practical concerns. Smuggle me from realms of capitalist separation. Slip me into the liminal magical realism of childhood—of family, community, carefree candlelit nights, and endless summer days. Magic realities that turn isolating towers to perfect climbing branches. Reminders that community is only a windy day away. In the stillness of a few minutes or hours, your microcosm can burst into mine.

The Idle Hour

Spread out a blanket on soft grass
Away from clocks that make time's passage crass

Feel wind's silken slither across your face
Watch clouds rush by at industrious pace

Let solid earth absorb the weight of things undone
Wait for your skin to tingle and tighten in the sun

Listen to frogs croak and birds coo
Right now they have more cares than you

You're simply here to breathe in the power
Of the idle hour

Poignant Pigments

The US is a graphite sketch
Adolescent landmarks and newborn borders
Drawn in straight state lines
Amnesiac monochrome of millennial gray
Bleeds uniformity into morality
Brands scarcity as necessity
Masquerades permanence
On paper crumpled with erased past

Mexico is an oil painting
   Where past and present collide
      In vast curves and crests of pigment
      Canvas saturated in cultural layers
   Movement of ancient brushstrokes
Visible beneath fresh vividness

Deep blue-green of banyan-lined cenotes
   Burnt sienna cave drawings
      Sun-bleached beige building blocks
         Of civilizations gone by

      Pink marble of European imperialism
     Red blood of change seeped into soil over eons
   Red, white, and green of freedom
For some

Orange, purple, and yellow of artisans' arthritic fingers
   Dusty brown of wind racing sweat down laborers' backs

    Carefree blue of children splashing in fountains
   And sunshine yellow of friendships formed
Against steadfast cerulean ocean

Rainbow Día de los Muertos skulls
   White teeth against sun-browned skin
In smiles of descendants

How can I go back to a world delineated
In black and white
After living in aching, vibrant color?

Bridge to Ithaca

Ancient tomes whose golden calligraphy never fades. Stone cathedrals of learning captivate incoming classes' freshly freed eyes. Wavy paned windows frosted with defended wisdom next to sleek steel construction shining with childhood's brazen courage. Between dead knowledge and living curiosity. Between cicada echoes. Between tendrils of antique lamplight beckoning through fog that shrinks the world into my embrace. Magic. Between leaving everything and everyone I knew and becoming what I am, I met her. A girl with moonbeam hair, who stood proud as a sunflower, and laughed like boots dancing through first snows. A sister whose soul mine instantly recognized, a best friend. As we ran, climbed, and giggled through the night. As we learned how to flirt with boys and pass exams, we were fearless. Royalty. Princesses of academia, of the tiny kingdom of friends we formed. Friends who showed us secret ancient tunnels to crumbling dams. Who wove fairytales of lost art in dusty attics. Dripped ghost stories in damp cellars shaking with scenes only we could step into. Untouchable within our kind borders. Until she visited her family's distant lands, and never returned.

I went skinny dipping for the first time the summer after she died. Stripped bare between savage stone shores, between people who would never know her. Royalty no more. Our secret tunnel gorge a gash in our lovely lands torn asunder.

Ten years later, a healer told me when she looked at me, she saw death. That a piece of me was missing. She pressed needles into my skin. Tried to stitch my soul back into me. I never went back. Never asked if it worked. Would it be so bad if it didn't?

let my soul be bridge
to the Magic In Between
my Princess Laura

Ode to Possibility

A gaze that draws my eyes to your lips
    A voice I'd rub into my skin as perfume
One with no broken promises to eclipse
    No history to taint my desire's bloom
My eager mind forms your shadowy shape
    Pursue sacred sharing to make a sketch
        Who's your favorite philosopher or poet?
            Do you find life lush or ennui to escape?
    Will your ideas make my spirit shrink or stretch?
        What's your world look like, and your place in it?

I want to know how you'd hold my hair, my hands
    The sounds you'd make if I kissed your collarbone
How long we could love without demands
    How we'd fit together if we didn't sleep alone
Soft sheets of your beliefs silhouetting mine
    Start each morning licking acceptance into your skin
        Breathe hope and belonging into your lips
            Baring our souls, we'd step closer to the shared divine
    I thought and no one cared, therefore have I been?
    I'd be confident I Am in your cognizant grips

Loving freely cascades into desire to own
        Permanence with you seems a pretty embrace
Why wouldn't we shore our bond up in stone?
        Welcome tenderly to my tranquil cottage space
Smile at your shoes next to mine in our cramped castle
        Your sleep-rasped words would be my Sunday mass
                Rug-wrapped in front of the fireplace we'd lie
                        Plant your pocket ash as our front yard Yggdrasil
        Through aged diamond-paned stained glass
                We'd watch it bud and unfurl to meet the sky

But perhaps it'd grow a bit too delightedly
        Our lovely view obstructed by cluttering leaves
We tended its first fruits so excitedly
        But what was once freely given, now it thieves
Continuous crops left my soil depleted
        My land needed to lie fallow, not sustain life
                Drenching floods leave my dusty dirt unquenched
                        How could our world-spanning roots be safely seated?
        Outside a—CRASH—Fear pierces me warm as a knife
                I chase dubious sound, desperation-drenched

Wrench open the door, sure that I'll see
        Our grand love felled to branched barricade
But there in the yard still proudly stands our tree
        Pressed against the trunk, fear fades in ash shade
I contemplate our cottage, free and inviolate
        Except the gouges the last love left in the thatch
                And have those cracks in the foundation spread?
                        Clouds coalesce to darken my environ wet
        Inside place metal pots for rain the roof can't catch
                Rest a bucket on my stomach in our damp bed

My arms form a dread-dripped hollow plastic drum
    Conductorless chorus of metal splashes surround
To wet plaster our sanctuary succumbs
    Heart sinking in mushy mattress—I recall the ground
Push aside the pots, roll back the braided rug
    That concealed the hateful cracks buried beneath
        Roots wriggle through like worms to the storm
            Curl around my ankles, to the holes I'm drug
    Trees are meant to make it easier to breathe
        But this mildewed air won't give my lungs form

Dug in softened hardwood, torn fingernails withstand
    Kick, claw, and scrabble my desperate escape
Outside hands and knees fall to dirt, vacuum lungs expand
    And contract—panic permeates the sunny landscape
Halt!—Our attraction and ruination still abstract
    Race to pull your open palms from my poisoned plot
        Close your unplanted samara seed safely in hand
            Empty, my compromised cottage remains intact
    Parcel up nascent affection with decisive knot
        My ash-dusted gift—Freedom to find more fertile land

I won't ever hold you through late-night lonely fears
    Or trace morning-gold sun streams down to your soul
Won't count each open smile the last before tears
    Wait for one of our needs to swallow the other whole
In my vacant space, I'll breathe in my own air
    Wind will swirl your samara seeds to worthy love
        Stopped at quickening untested fertility
            Ethereal, diffused dreams never cede to despair
Amorphous wish as aurora borealis above
        We get to stay a fantasy, a perfect possibility

Syrupy Syllables Drip from Your Lips

My name lingers on your fingertips
Falls frequently from your lips

Whispered more when you slip near
Than it's else wise kissed my ears all year

On your tongue, each syllable sticks
Slow at the curves as cold honey drips

By request your voice is loved best
Breath held on sonorous shiver and rest

With secret glances and a gentle, "Molly"
You press my sense back into me

Missing You

I am my moon's last opal drop
Gliding down your dawn grass blade
Gravity grasp your growth to stop
Bow your back for me displayed

You call me with each cicada scream
My voice aches along echoes to reach you
Yes I drowned our discordant dream
View our silenced beauty through murky blue

Charged needles carve out my center
Spin in relation to your magnetic field
To this current I long to surrender
But my momentum will not yield

My waters must return to my oceans
I cannot stay in your summer lands
Don't doubt the depth of my devotions
By how I drip from your desperate hands

When cycles of discovery and concealment convene
Clear eyes belie a body full of things unnamed
Where life ancient and fragile swims unseen
My tides are endless, lapping—death untamed

You, the sun, dance jewels on my waves
I welcome your piercing rays of light
But creatures without eyes wend ways
Through my caves of eternal night

My shallows race to your warm sand embrace
Each time I can't bear to leave once more
My moon calls me back to deep sea grace
I will always beckon stronger than the shore

Wheel of Attrition

Soul carved from smoke by granite embrace
Sun's meager ray turns endless night gray
My destiny dances in your embers of grace

Born shadow with no wrongness to displace
Pour my darkness to dirt, slake me to clay
Soul carved from smoke by granite embrace

From boneless dust, to life's sacred vase
Wedge my warm self, mold me your way
My destiny dances in your embers of grace

Press fingerprint pattern to skin like silk lace
Perfect pottery needs no voice to pray
Soul carved from smoke by granite embrace

Imperfections glare in your mirror glow face
Fragile porcelain frozen by fire to obey
My destiny dances in your embers of grace

Failed creation shattered without trace
Scattered in your hallowed shadow to stay
Soul carved from smoke by granite embrace
My destiny dances in your embers of grace

Kind of Love

I've known love, or at least the words "I love you"
Learned most loves aren't something to pursue
There are so many types, you see
So many ways to lose pieces of me

There's the loving me on your terms and time
When I make it easy and sublime
I bend till I creak to meet your needs
While you pretend you can't hear my pleas
Kind of love

There's the valuing me as a symbol of your status
Our happiness an afterthought to how they view us
Pretending to appreciate all my chaotic colors
Then painting over them so I'm palatable for others
Kind of love

The putting me up on a pedestal
Until looking up makes you feel small
So you cut me down to size
Because of the two of us, you're really the prize
Kind of love

The seeming to love me for me
Then wanting to change me entirely
Prune back pieces of my soul till I'm reformed
Less resilient, less wild, more conveniently conformed
Kind of love

The showing sacred vulnerability
To secure my guarantee
That everything you lack I'll be
Your need growing so great I'll never be free
Kind of love

The holding on tight with a python squeeze
If I could fill my lungs, I might use that breath to leave
Isolate me from my family and friends
Leave no one else to hold, so our embrace never ends
Kind of love

I'm tired of loves that always leave me with less
Leave months of clearing debris to clean up the mess
Deciding which pieces are too shattered for the rebuilding phase
Under loads once held lightly, my weakened structure sways

I want love that leaves me stronger than ever before
When I feel trapped, builds me a new door
That opens the windows to shine light on my face
When our love outgrows, we build a new place

Can expand as we do, free of fear
Its depth never used to make me or you disappear
In baring my myriad natures for you, I see myself clearly
With each self you give, I cherish more dearly
Kind of love

Your sleeping face is the most beautiful thing I've seen
No matter how tired, I'll always let you rest while I clean
I'd know your laugh if I didn't hear it for fifty years
All of your smiles are my favorite souvenirs
Kind of love

As I change, you learn to love each version of me
Burrowing and growing into your favorite climbing tree
You can't know where the next page will lead
But the story of us is your favorite to read
Kind of love

The only relationships you'd ever stand between
Are the ones hurting me in ways I haven't yet seen
My goals are as important to you as your own
No matter the obstacle, you don't face it alone
Kind of love

Believe in each other when we can't believe in ourselves
In a lifetime collecting memories and seashells for our shelves
When I lack energy to love both of us well, I always choose you
Because loving you is my favorite thing to do
Kind of love

Not half of a whole that can't survive on its own
But greater and more yourself than you've ever known
Not barrier or weight between me and the world
But transport to all the best things, wings unfurled
Kind of love

A love so great, these bodies, goals, memories it transcends
And greets me in the next when this lifetime ends

Helen of Troy

Your first sunlit smile as night retreats west
Stretch as slumber recedes, fingers and toes pointing
Hide your morning breath in kisses to my chest
Bounce to the bathroom, return with minty tongue anointing

Wild curls tangling with white sheet
Laughter and freedom of your body against mine
Lay in front of fire as wool-wrapped toes heat
Fingers steepling around tea, protective as pine

Needles soft under your fearless forest gait
You outshine Mother Moon's luminescence
Even the sea agrees, her pull isn't so great
The very mountains can't compete with your presence

If the swirling winds dare rise up against you
I'll always be there to hold your dress down
My Marilyn, leave the presidents to their coups
Let's twirl through every golden age and town

I'd not war over or with you to the end, instead
From stained glass build you an altar sublime
Set aside that snake, come back to bed
My Cleopatra, those Romans aren't worth the time

Freeze in honeyed amber this perfect joy
Your form and mine cozily curled
Safe from gods and kings, my Helen of Troy
The most beautiful woman in the world

Unnamed

Blessed with beauty and called from clay to life
Perfect Pandora, gifted to Epimetheus as wife
If only the gods had given her heart and humility
Instead of her evil box and cursèd curiosity

Dahut the sorcerous sinner couldn't contain her lust
Her father, pious king of Ys, kindly gave his trust
Betrayed at her lover's request to steal his key
And foolishly throw open the gates to the sea

Created from the same clay as man in equality
Lilith's defiance got her written out of history
Adam offered up a rib for a woman who'd heed him
But Eve's fervid greed couldn't remain in Eden

Punishments, demons, seductresses, sirens
Succubi, gorgons, harpies, morgens
They take a good man and ruin all he could be
Bring the fall of man; sink kingdoms beneath the sea

....but what if that's not the whole story

Pandora was bound to a husband named for "hindsight"
His purpose was failed foil to his brother's "foresight"
But Prometheus's prescience didn't save him from Zeus's ire
Eternally tortured for granting mankind the gift of fire

Permanently punished man with Pandora's box of woe
But why did vengeful Zeus need a middle woman though?
He was well known as a petty, jealous god-king on high
To pin his sin on Pandora, let's at least have a convincing lie

Every sickness and hardship flowing from box to countryside
But we can survive it all because of the lone hope still inside
So which is it? Do we have what's inside or out?
Does her box serve a point? What's this fucking story about?

Dahut wasn't the first villain in Ys's tragic tale
And in shifting the blame, it lost one crucial detail
It's clear that her *many* lovers met the same twisted fate
But not how *one* woman could bear the weight of a great sea gate

At least Dahut got a mention with the slut shaming and blame
Lot's wife got turned to salt and didn't even get a name
None of Noah's women were mentioned when god cleared the map
His son, Ham, got in for watching his wine-drunk naked nap

Lilith is called Mother of Demons, if she's mentioned at all
Eve is the gullible corruptress, blamed for man's downfall
Lilith's crime was refusing to submit to Adam in every dispute
In god's lovingly planted paradise, Eve's was trying the fruit?

It's common to say, "Not if he was the last man on earth!"
But no one seems to comment on the first man's worth
If all the women in creation leave paradise to escape you
Perhaps you have some introspection to do

If subservience is a defining female birthright
Its absence in our first women seems a divine oversight
But Adam never earned their respect, in fact
His only trait was the knowledge he lacked

Though they call themselves lover, father, king, or creator
They must be cast aside, if their true name is Dictator
Perhaps I should hope our matriarchs are guilty as they say
Instead of clearing prehistoric crimes, emulate them today

Maybe the downfall of Man isn't such an evil thing
When the uprising of Woman has such a hopeful ring

A Poet in Kentucky

For Lee Pennington and Kratz Place

Home filled with centuries of love and wonder
Cozy cottage, retired tavern, and grand manor
Paintings, tapestries, masks, artifacts, and books
Medieval royal bench next to a hot tub for she who looks
Time is a poet in Kentucky

In his good works his bed is dressed
He wears the world on his chest
Knows no two leaves are the same green
And your words have power the universe has never seen
Kindness is a poet in Kentucky

His beard as true as his word
Smile as easy as the breeze to the bird
Students old as the trees and young as the frost
Slip through forgotten eras and sit happily lost
To learn what befell King Arthur if they're lucky
Magic is a poet in Kentucky

Imbas Forosnai

Seeped across the seas from their father's land
    Or traded from the aes sídhe for his native name
    Creep with Brontës' banshee on barren cliffs to stand
Terrible beauty beyond frosted pane waits to wail her claim
    Blends lullaby with lament with moor windborne idea
    Till frigid wildness lives in their souls' flickering flame
Maybe Melpomene turned nursemaid to brilliant young Maria
    Tragic care turned clear eyes and poetic spirit wan
    Divine inspiration couldn't be her panacea
She split her gifts to bless Charlotte, Emily, and Anne
    To heart, soul, and mind what one girl couldn't bear
    The expanding god-spark to depart the world of man
And create the kingdoms of Angria and Gondal where
    Toy soldiers live the lows of lost love and joined minds lofted high
    Though the grave ivy tugs at them as long as they stay there
Always they long for heather heaths beneath their foggy sky
    Where sídhe sob at snowy windows to be let in from the moor
    Ice-cold hands clutch death beside imbas forosnai

The Great Migration pulls millions with freedom's lure
    Flee phoenix burnt to ash on Jim Crow cotton field
    Fly along sparked steel tracks for futures to procure
Toward city within city by Anansi's web concealed
    From brownstone to jazz band he spun his gut strings
    But his cunning wife deserves credit for every story revealed
From Aso's Dark Tower, reborn stars soar with flaming wings
    With invitation and a nominal fee, zoot-suited Eshu lets you in
    Euterpe's triumph keys swirl into the twilight Ethel sings
To join smoke-curl magic of promising minds mingling within
    The Joy Goddess of Harlem stirs community like cocktails
    Defies mere mortals to mix worlds in seraphic sin
Zora and Nora dance on heels warm from blazed trails
    Langston and Mami Wati whisper rivers that outlast stone
    WEB De Bois and Br'er Rabbit smoke cigars and swap tales
High John laughs at common trash so unjustly on the throne
    While Wallace and Countee create quietly in the corner
    Zora leaves to heed the ceaseless claim of ancestors' unknown
Joins the unnamed dead till someone comes to mourn her
    Their music and words remain, though every party must end
    The Dark Tower shutters and Euterpe waits for her next performer

To the Lower East Side, she and sister Erato descend
        Let rooms in the Chelsea where rent's paid in art
        At the doors the rules and pace of society suspend
In the smoking embers of phoenix's tumultuous depart
        Cold-handed, empty-stomached artist spirits find refuge
        For every vacancy, Erato finds a wildly yearning heart
On Leonard and Janis, Sid and Nancy love falls as deluge
        Some devotions stop your lungs younger than consumption
        The call Patti, Allen, Arthur, and Andy could not refuse
When one pen stops, time tenses for another's assumption
        Across time and space, seas and history's separation
        As soon as one circle burns out, another blazes in eruption

From Bloomsbury Group to Plato's Academy to Lost Generation
        From Florentine Renaissance to Russian Silver Age
        From Alexandrian poets to Sappho's first circle of creation
When the phoenix has died in all the wars we wage
        And your poet's soul is the last left on soil ashed infertile
        Bring your best words to hidden, dusty local stage
When indifference to art seems universal
        The pen the most painful, pointless path to choose
        Ignite the flame of your creative circle
Eternal tenth muse

Larger Than Time

On your tiptoes, you see into the top drawer
Without training wheels, ride faster than before
Your mom wrote notes on the backs of recipes
But you have plentiful paper and public libraries
You can read beyond your shore

On scholarships and love, you leave home
With planes, and trains, and internet to roam
Your world is larger than your parents' ever grew
You look afar, unafraid of those unlike you
You can add their wisdom to your own

Towards goals lovingly granted you reach and race
Trace the path with an ever-increasing pace
Only to find when you arrive, that your life feels untrue
Maybe these aspirations weren't meant for you
You can build a new place

Actions and anxieties searched behind
Evaluate each unmapped territory you find
For pains and passions yours to retain
And which don't fit the terrain of your brain
You can expand your mind

You're more you with each passing year
The more you become, the less you fear
Your works proceed you, influence expands
Life and love grow wider than the lands
You can draw others near

The world changes in ways no one controls
Life-led adventures eclipse outgrown goals
Though your list of lost loves grows long
You don't rage against change to belong
You can fulfill countless roles

Decades seem to have passed in a wink
Your body and world begin to shrink
Drain of daily pains and pills has grown
Gentled by all the beauty you've known
You can hold past and present in sync

In photos, you don't seem small and old
Your presence looms large, a gift to behold
Walls speak a lifetime of distinguished medals
Your heart sings the poetry of passing petals
You are the love leading out from the cold

You're as vulnerable as the first breath of life
As bold as the kindness that ends strife

As curious as ancient questions, asked across time
As humble as the ache at the end of the climb

You're as brief as first light's flame in morning dew
As eternal as countless souls sharing the story of you

The love and joy you embody remind us
We can live larger than hope, and smaller than kindness

Firefly Walks

Fog curls around curves in the road
Steamed rain seeps from asphalt to soles
Distant toads croak in secret code
Senses steeped in our summer strolls

Fireflies float from wildflowers
Twilight talks touch fading sunset
Mom and me, rich in golden hours
Silhouettes sink into velvet vignette

Cicada symphony echoes across skin
Pulse reverberates with the call
Desperate to freeze us within
Summer nights' fleeting magic thrall

Mom says, "Fall makes you feel old
And spring makes you young"
Summer makes me tighten my hold
To short firefly weeks, forever clung

"I'm going to live to four hundred"
State the intention for my body to know
Would so much time turn life's joys sundrid?
Mom would rather current connection grow

Please senses, don't succumb to slumber
Linger and listen to laughter of trees
Mystery of juniper and cucumber
Scent snagged on fragment of breeze

Water spark of iced lemon on soft lips
Swallow it down until stomach is full
Skin sucks at heavy air in hot sips
But still thirsts for the night's pull

White petals glow upon backdrop of dusk
Savor while the sun's last rays pour
Lungs lap at air's perfumed musk
Gasp to always feel and know more

See lamplight stretch for distant star gleam
Eyes clutch at colors only birds perceive
Bursting in ever present, nameless dream
We want senses humans cannot conceive

See heat lightning set pink clouds ablaze
And feel it like only the sky knows
An ice cold stream wending its ways
Split shocking through our toes

Feel home begging with magnetic force
To seasons that flow in our bones' hollows
Voices vibrate out and back to source
Whole shadow world of shapes to swallow

Gyroscope of our spines please spin
Our pink paw pads to ground
Let us know weather in our skin
Before distant thunder makes a sound

Let us love the earth resting in our roots
And the wind playing tag in our leaves
Each corner of else and us in cahoots
Ever yearning new ways to perceive

Ageless forest cat joins our walk
Cul-de-sac sage with one milky eye
Screams have replaced his silent stalk
Can no longer hear his own cry

My mom bends to scoop him
He looks so small in her arms
Though his ears and eyes dim
Nature calmed by the night's charms

We wonder how long his mind can stay
While his body releases its hold
Failing senses the precious price we pay
For making it marvelously alive to old

Mom can't see orange rings round moon
And the stars don't twinkle for her tonight
Fire sprites will blink back to their realm soon
No one gets to gaze forever at their light

We track back home with fall on heel
Still walls force wild immensity in chest
Unforgiving fluorescent shards reveal
I've been too busy becoming to rest

Amidst this lush life my panic arises
Summer will soon pass and I've not saved
Enough of the fireflies' gold to irises
Nor felt growth ring on spine engraved

Didn't braid blossoms into sun-bleached hair
Or encode the stars in new freckles
Didn't float enough in the lake without care
Or map mudcracks to pruned feet wrinkles

Night's calls for autumn grow heady
Urgently soak in summer as asphalt
Warmth disappears before I'm ready
Pulse speeds as heart bids time to halt

My mom says she still sees fireflies
But I haven't seen them in weeks
Until I learn they fly earlier as day dies
Race to behold brilliant dwindling streaks

They say "too much of a good thing"
But on the vibrant bruise of life
I press for purple pain's siren ring
Let insatiable vitality burn rife

For one more sunset or four centuries
I will blend every defeat with more tries
I will break up the dark with my stories
Find me, eyes sparkling, with the fireflies

Parents' Poems

Molly

Roses are red, Violets are blue
I'm sending this because we miss you

We will see you soon at the end of May
We can't wait to we get to that day

will throw you a party you'll have a blast
The memory of it will forever last.

Tell your friends we miss them to
use the money to go buy a brew.

Love
Mom & Dad

Molly

Roses are red
violets are blue
here are some sweets for you

I hope everything is going well
when we see you it sure will be swell

I know soon you will be some place nice
until then Buffalo will have to suffice

We will see you soon
and we all will be cheerful

Until then my lovely daughter please be
careful.

Love
Mom + Dad
XXXXX
OOO OO
XXXXX
OOOOO

Molly,

- Daddy just had surgery

- and I did too

- So we got your Valentine
out late so don't be blue

- The candle was made with
our love just for you

Love
Mom & Dad
XOXOXOXOXO

P.S. Sorry for my lame rhyme.
It is nothing short of a crime.

Mom
XOXO

Molly

Roses are Red, Violets are Blue
The airport got one, but you made two.

Use these gifts night or day
They will always brighten your way.

I hope the little one gives you a thrill
you know I think you a real special girl.

Tim Dahl

The bucket is color: Turquoise waters
smell: Twisted citrus + spice.

Mully mully what can I say
you brighten each and every day.

You books are good and reading is fun
Someday you'll have a number (one)

Eat some candy even just a few
Someday you know all your dreams will come true

An closing I just want to say
mom & Dad love you every day

Love
Mom & Dad

X X X X X
O O O O O
X X X X X
O O O O O

Molly ♡

Roses are red, violets are blue
your poems and stories are good too

Having you home is such a delight
we get along great & never fight

I know you will be gone someday
& hope you find a place to laugh & play

Hope today you enjoy the sun
go outside and have some fun

Love Dad
OOOO
XXXX
OOOO
XXXX

Acknowledgements

This debut poetry collection, and all my creative endeavors, exist because of the generous love, teaching, and collaboration of so many people. First and foremost, my family. From the dedication at the beginning to their poems at the end, this book is bursting with the love, safety, and inspiration my parents provide. They created a beautiful world for me—one worth fighting for and rhyming about.

I have immense gratitude for my best friend and fellow poet, Kayla Nichols. We navigated the process of publishing our first collections together, and I couldn't have chosen a better person to untangle the myriad details with me. If you enjoyed this book, especially our braided poem MAIDENMOTHERCRONE, I encourage you to read her gorgeous collection, The Stuff of Stars.

This project wouldn't exist on this timeline, and certainly not at this quality, without Kayla and the other incredibly talented poets in our critique group. Thank you to The Philosopher's House for hosting us and for being a pillar of intentional community and creative togetherness in our little city.

I would have never started up the steep and overgrown path of poetry without people like Lee Pennington pruning the way. Thank you for the foreword, thank you for believing in me, thank you for inspiring and impressing upon generations of students that our verse-shaped hearts are worth sharing.

Thank you to all my loved ones for being living poetry. I wouldn't have the fortitude to confront the darkness, or the expansiveness to see the light, without you.

Lastly, thank you to my readers. Writing, creating—just existing—through late-stage capitalism can be profoundly isolating, and the ability to connect—soul to page to soul—with you is the most meaningful way I know to Be.

130

About the Author

Molly Ann McDonough is a poet and fiction author whose work explores hope as active resistance, sacred love, and the threads that tie everyday lives into a communal story woven with mythic meaning. Her writing draws on lyric and literary feminist traditions, offering magic and mirth not as escape, but as a way of retuning the heart toward the beauty that lives alongside hardship.

Her debut poetry collection, *Hope in Hateful Times* (2026), centers community, resilience, and the divine feminine in the face of injustice. Her short fiction has appeared in science fiction and fantasy anthologies, and her debut fantasy novel, *A World Apart*, is forthcoming in 2026.

A neurodivergent, multidisciplinary thinker, Molly brings the same curiosity and devotion to her writing that she brings to her life. When she isn't writing, she can usually be found coding, reading, appreciating the humans she is lucky to spend her life with, or telling her cat, Pickle, that she is the most perfect being in the whole universe.

Find more of her work at www.mollyannmcdonough.com.

Reviews and word-of-mouth recommendations mean the world to indie authors. If you enjoyed *Hope in Hateful Times*, please consider leaving a review on your favorite platform or exploring Molly's other works.

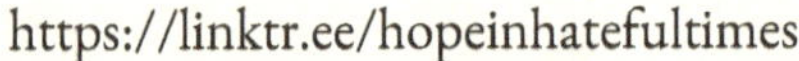

https://linktr.ee/hopeinhatefultimes